Failing Well

A Short Guide for Organisations and Individuals

Caris E Grimes

Copyright © 2021 Caris E Grimes

First published 2021 by Sarah Grace Publishing,
an imprint of Malcolm Down Publishing Ltd
www.malcolmdown.co.uk

24 23 22 21 20   7 6 5 4 3 2 1

The right of Author Name to be identified as the author
of this work has been asserted by him in accordance
with the Copyright, Designs and Patents Act 1988.

British Library Cataloguing in Publication Data
A catalogue record for this book is available from the British Library.
ISBN 978-1-912863-85-3

Cover design by Esther Kotecha
Art direction by Sarah Grace

Printed in the UK

Contents

Introduction

Failures and mistakes are an inevitable part of our lives, both personally and professionally. They are also an inevitable part of the life of any organisation. As a surgeon, I wanted to know how I could use my failures to become better at my job in the same way that I want to learn from my errors to become a better friend, a better wife, a better mum, etc. As I began to take on roles within clinical governance in the hospital, I was keen to understand how the hospital as an organisation or any organisation could learn from things that don't go well. As I started reading about this, I began to realise that the things I was learning were generic and could apply to any person or organisation in a wide range of different circumstances.

This short booklet has been adapted from a webinar. It uses examples from business, entrepreneurs, parenting, education, healthcare and science to demonstrate the breadth of these issues and allow readers to understand how broad these things are and how many situations the same principles can be applied to. For a slightly longer and personal account, please see my book, *Failing Intelligently*.

Key Points:

- We learn more from our failures than our successes
- But failure in itself does not automatically lead to learning
- People and organisations can either fail well or they can fail badly
- Learning to fail well leads to versatility, adaptability and resilience
- Learning to fail well early in life or early in your career can lead to long-term success
- Both individual and organisational factors impact on whether a failure results in an individual and organisation failing well or failing badly

The Benefits and Liabilities of Failure and Success

In the 1960s, Cyert and March wrote about how organisations can learn more from their failures than they can their successes.[3,4] This was unpacked further by Sitkin in 1992 and others have built on it since.[5] What Sitkin argued was that there are benefits of success. We know this because we all like success. It increases motivation, it increases satisfaction and it increases confidence. It reduces hesitation and second thoughts. It reduces inefficiency by getting rid of suboptimal ways of doing things. So, if something doesn't work, you don't do it. It promotes stability and short-term performance.

But there are liabilities to being successful. You can become complacent. You can develop a reduced motivation to adapt, change or pursue new approaches and this is important because we live in a world that changes – nothing stays the same all the time. You see in evolution that the "survival of the fittest" is about the ability to change and adapt to changing environments and the problem with being successful through sticking to the same routines is that there may not be a perceived need to adapt or change. Those who have repeated success may avoid doing anything new for fear it may not be as good as what is already done. Success can lead to inertia and to rigid ways of doing things on the assumption that if things continue exactly the same, success will continue. But it is very rare in life that things do continue exactly the same. Environments and situations change and develop constantly.

Sitkin also argued that there are benefits to failure. It can foster a willingness to experiment and try new things. It increases resilience. It challenges the status quo. It draws attention to an issue, and it challenges us to think and reflect deeply on a problem. We need to be creative. We may need to try something different. We may need to look at the problem in a different way. He further argued that small failures and near misses were more useful to learn from because when there is a large failure, the first thing we try to do is limit the damage and not necessarily prioritise working out what happened and why. Therefore, these organisational approaches to large failures tend to be protective rather than exploratory.

Ultimately, if you only ever succeed, then this can foster reliability, but it can lead to long-term failure. But failure, if approached intelligently, fosters resilience, adaptability and versatility and this in itself can lead to long-term success.

Failing Well and Failing Badly

People and organisations can either fail well or fail badly. If an incident is managed well, people and the organisation they are in will fail well. They will learn and adapt as a result of the failure, understand the fault lines in their processes and increase their resilience. Ultimately, they will grow more successful.

However, people and organisations too often fail badly. The impact of an incident or failure instead results in blame, failure to take responsibility, and ultimately, a failure to really understand why something has happened and learn from it in a way that allows both the organisation and the individual to learn and grow.

Both organisations and individuals therefore need to develop a strategy to fail well.

Fixed and Growth Mindsets

If you have a child in education, you may have come across the concept of growth mindset pioneered by Carol Dweck.[4] This argues simply that there are two types of people. There are 'fixed mindset' people and 'growth mindset' people. You may recognise the characteristics of each of these in yourself, friends, family or colleagues. It is quite a simplistic but useful way of looking at things, but it's not without its critics.

Characteristics of a fixed mindset include people who are defined by their failures or successes. They see their skills as something they are born with and not something they can change. They believe that they are either good at something or they aren't. Therefore, challenges can be something to avoid because they may reveal a lack of skill or ability and there can be a tendency to give up easily. Effort is unnecessary and something you do if you aren't good enough i.e., you don't have enough natural ability. If you give a fixed mindset person critical feedback, you may find that they get quite defensive and take it personally, because they are defined by their success or failure. When setbacks happen, they tend to blame others and they get discouraged.

However, characteristics of a growth mindset include people who perceive that their skills can come through hard work. Obviously, there is sometimes a degree of natural talent, but all very successful people have had to work hard even when they have natural ability. They hold the view that they can always improve and therefore challenges can be an opportunity to learn and grow as well as develop persistence. Effort is viewed as essential and is the path to mastery of a skill. Growth mindset people tend to ask for feedback. They see it as a useful way of learning as it will identify areas that others can see need improvement. Setbacks are therefore seen as a wake-up call to either try harder next time, do something different or find ways around the problem.

The issue is this: Fixed mindset people tend to fail badly. They give up easily, they blame others and they try not to take responsibility. Whereas growth mindset people tend to fail well. They persevere, they take responsibility and they demonstrate learning.

But that is not the whole story because it is not just about the individual, it is also about the environment or culture that they are working or living in. We will come back to the environmental and cultural factors.

Most of the research around growth mindset has been in education. There is evidence that developing a growth mindset in children leads to a long-term improvement in their grades, they are more likely to take challenging subjects, it may influence their future career success because they are not afraid of challenge and there is less impact of failure on self-esteem, self-worth and self-confidence.

Failure is seen as defining a person in a fixed mindset but seen as separate from the individual and a tool to learn from in a growth mindset.

A Few Research Highlights

An interesting paper from education was published by Destin et al where the researchers divided parents into a control group and an intervention group.[6] In the intervention group, they taught parents how to respond positively to their children's failures. They then looked at what happened with the children and they demonstrated that those with parents in the intervention group performed significantly better in subsequent academic tests than those with parents in the control group. When a child fails, the parent helps the child work harder, look at strategies, identify ways around or through the problem.

Another study showed that parents behave differently towards their children depending on whether they view their child's failure as "debilitating" or "enhancing".[7] Therefore, if you want your child to have a growth mindset, you need to have an "enhancing" attitude towards your child's failures rather than a "debilitating" attitude. It is more important how you react to a child's failures than it is how you react to their successes. A debilitating attitude means that you worry about your child's ability, pity your child if they fail and try to comfort your child for not having enough ability. An enhancing attitude means that you focus on effort and strategies and express the view that your child can improve. If you teach the parents how to have an enhancing attitude, then the children are more likely to have a growth mindset.

Another interesting study published in Nature studied junior scientists applying for National Institute of Health R01 grants.[8] It took people who were early in their career and looked at the ones that narrowly missed obtaining a grant (near misses) against the ones who were narrowly successful (narrow wins). They studied what happened over the next ten years. They looked at the number of junior scientists who dropped out of the system and never applied for another grant, they looked at the total number of papers they published, at the number of "hit" papers published (which they defined as being in the top 5% of citations in the same year and field) and they look at the average number of citations in the same year and field.

What they found was that although there was not much difference in the total number of papers published over the next ten years, the failures (near misses) significantly outperform the successes (narrow wins) in the number of hit papers published at both five years and ten years. The same thing happens when they looked at the average number of citations per paper at five years and ten years – those that failed at the start of their career significantly outperform the early successes.

The authors concluded that although a failure or a near-miss at the beginning of a junior scientist's career predicted a 10% drop out rate, those that persisted significantly outperformed the narrow wins (successes) over the next five and ten years. They concluded that an "early career setback appears to cause a performance improvement for those who persevere". In other words, learning to fail well predicts long-term future success.

Psychological Safety

Failing well or failing badly is not just about the individual. It is also about the environment or culture that the individual is in. We can be the most growth-mindset individual in the institution, but if you have an institution where any admission of mistake will lead to blame, accusation and irreparable damage to your reputation, you are not going to admit to anything much.

Psychological safety is a concept which can be defined as a shared belief that the team is safe for interpersonal risk taking. It can be defined as "being able to show and employ oneself without fear of negative consequences to self-image, status or career". Professor Amy Edmondson, who pioneered the concept, states this:

> "At some point during elementary school, children start to recognise that what others think of them matters and they learn how to lower the risk of rejection or scorn . . . By the time we are adults, we're usually really good at it! Don't want to look ignorant? Don't ask questions. Don't want to look incompetent? Don't admit to mistakes. Don't want to be called disruptive? Don't make suggestions."[9]

It is argued that in psychologically safe teams, businesses and organisations, a culture is created where it's ok to ask questions, it's ok to admit to mistakes and it's ok to make suggestions because this is how we all learn and improve. If you have an organisation where these things are not possible, then you have an organisation that will not learn and therefore, by implication, is more likely to fail badly.

Human Factors

The issue here, both in our personal lives as well as our professional lives, is that none of us wake up in the morning with the intention of causing harm. In the same way that I don't wake up with the intention of arguing with my husband, overreacting to my kids or scraping the metalwork of the car, I don't intend to make a poor decision at work which will impact on my patient.

"Human factors" is the relationship between human beings and the systems with which they interact by focusing on improving efficiency, creativity, productivity and job satisfaction, with the goal of minimizing errors.[10] It is used in healthcare to improve patient safety but has also been used in a number of other industries including aviation, manufacturing and the military.

For example, the acronym IM SAFE (illness, medication, stress, alcohol, fatigue, emotion) that was developed in the aviation industry is useful as a self-assessment technique to determine when entering the workplace each day whether a person is safe for work. We also know that all these things will impact on our ability to build and maintain relationships and perform activities in any setting.

As surgeons, we need to be aware of our own "non-technical" skills.[11] These include situation awareness – we can get too focussed on what we are doing and not notice what is going on around us. Decision-making – which involves understanding the problem and then choosing the most appropriate response out of the possible options. This can be most difficult in emergency situations where big decisions on complex patients have to be made rapidly, often without all the information we might usually wish to have to make such a decision. Communication – being able to communicate well is at least a part of ensuring that you have understood what someone has told you and that you have been understood. Too often mistakes arise because someone assumes that someone else will do something or has done something. Team working – it's almost impossible to provide good patient care unless individuals are able to work well as a team, both within a clinical group and across disciplines and professions.

The Swiss Cheese model conceptualises safety and harm in a series of layers, or slices of Emmental cheese.[12] Each layer of safety, or slice, is not perfect – it has holes in it. However, with enough layers you can stop something passing all the way through the holes from one side to another. If we take the spreading of the Covid-19 virus as an example, then there are a number of human factor layers that can stop the virus spreading between two people. These include hand hygiene, avoiding touching your face, wearing masks, keeping space between people, complying with regulations about social distancing and crowds. With a "hole" in one of these, then the others may stop the spread of the virus. So, if you don't wash your hands, but conform to all the other layers, then it is unlikely the virus spreads. When holes in a number of layers line up, this causes an incident – someone who doesn't wash hands, touches their face, doesn't wear a mask, does not keep space and does not conform to any rules about crowds and distancing is highly likely to give the virus to someone else.

Acceptable and Unacceptable Failure

When businesses and organisations talk about learning from failure, they often proudly talk about acceptable failure. Google says they reward failure because it shows that their employees are experimenting and trying new things. But in healthcare, we tend to deal with unacceptable failure, such as avoidable death. Nor is it as simple as saying something is an acceptable failure or something is an unacceptable failure – there is a whole spectrum between the two, as demonstrated in Figure 1.

Figure 1: Acceptable and unacceptable failure adapted from Edmondson et al[13]

Most "Blame-worthy"	
Deviance	An individual chooses to violate a prescribed process or practice
Inattention	An individual inadvertently deviates from specifications
Lack of Ability	An individual doesn't have the skills, conditions or training to execute the job
Process Inadequacy	A competent individual adheres to a prescribed but faulty or incomplete process
Task challenge	An individual faces a task too difficult to be executed reliably every time
Process Complexity	A process composed of many elements breaks down when it encounters novel interactions
Uncertainty	A lack of clarity about future events causes people to take seemingly reasonable actions that produce undesired results
Hypothesis testing	An experiment to prove that an idea or a design will succeed fails
Exploratory testing	An experiment conducted to expand knowledge and investigate a possibility leads to an undesired result
Most "Praise-worthy"	

It is said that James Dyson's failed more than 5000 times when designing his vacuum cleaner: he made more than 5,000 versions of the vacuum cleaner before he had one that worked really well. Nobody minds talking about this – it is an acceptable failure. In healthcare we tend to work with unacceptable failure, whereas the failures people prefer to talk about are the acceptable ones, the experimentation ones.

Therefore, we cannot underestimate the impact on someone involved in a significant failure, particularly an "unacceptable" failure. We see this in healthcare with incidents resulting in avoidable harm to a patient, but it is by no means unique to healthcare.

Impact

A study by Jason Cope on the experience of entrepreneurs shows that people involved in a significant failure go through several stages.[14] Firstly, they go through a period of significant loss. This can have effects financially, emotionally, physiologically, socially and professionally. They can suffer from loss of sleep, stress, depression, loss of reputation, stigmatisation, shame, remorse, humiliation, embarrassment, despair, loss of self-esteem and self-confidence. There can be impacts on professional networks and support, impact on finances and impact on close relationships, etc.

In a healthcare setting, when someone is involved in a failure, there is no-one who can blame or condemn them more than they will be blaming and condemning themselves. Therefore, a culture of blame is totally counter-productive and results in no learning – the individual is unable to learn and the organisation doesn't usually learn either. Both fail badly. What people in this phase needs is a lot of support, and especially peer support. Without the support, they will be unlikely to grow and learn from the incident. They will not be able to fail well. This is why culture is so important.

Secondly, Cope demonstrated that many individuals need a hiatus – they need a break from things for a bit. They need to get away from the situation in order to move from the emotional phase to the logical phase.

Finally, they enter a third phase of gradual recovery, rebuilding and learning. This occurs over time. Emotion precedes logic. It is in this phase that most of the learning occurs.

"Being held in high regard by other people, especially those with whom one interacts in an ongoing manner, is a strong fundamental human desire, and most people tacitly believe that revealing failure will jeopardise this esteem" Cannon & Edmondson 2005[2]

"Everybody gathered – the professors, all the consultants, everybody who was anybody threw in their pennyworth as to what I should have done and didn't do and had a better outcome . . . it was quite traumatic and humiliating. They weren't unkind, but just having your practice dissected in detail was quite difficult." (Obstetrician)[1]

When individuals are involved in failure, they often have severe feelings of shame, fear and humiliation and often suffer from loss of self-confidence, self-esteem and fear or actual loss of reputation. Again, unless they are supported, they are not going to be able to fail well. Support particularly from colleagues, but also friends and family is really very important.

When an incident happens in healthcare, one of three different outcomes may result to the individual involved.[15] Firstly, there may be an emotional crash, a significant impact on mental health, an inability to return to work and, at worst, suicide (failing badly). Secondly, the individual may avoid responsibility, fail to learn, blames others or may have a loss of confidence. They may return to work but may struggle (failing badly). Thirdly, and ideally, the individual seeks support, takes responsibility, learns from the failure, returns to work and improves as a result (failing well).

Whether an individual fails well or fails badly is dependent on individual factors such as the way they view themselves, their successes and their failures (mindset) but also the organisational or environmental factors, such as whether they have supportive colleagues, whether there is a negative or blame culture and whether there is a feeling of being gossiped about.

Fails Well or Fails Badly?

Individual factors	Organisational factors
E.g. Mindset	E.g. Lack of supportive colleagues Negative / Blame culture Feeling of being gossiped about

We need to get both right in order to really learn.

How to Manage Failure

If you are the one in the mess, or if you have a colleague who is, this is what you need to do:

1. **Honesty / Duty of Candour.** You need to start with being honest with yourself, your patients and their families (if you are in healthcare), your clients and your colleagues. In healthcare, we have a "Duty of Candour" which is a duty to tell the truth to the patient about what has happened, but you also need to tell the truth to your organisation.

2. **Seek support.** You need people – especially colleagues – who will surround you and will protect your reputation because people cannot fail well, they cannot become better at what they are doing, if their reputations and careers have been destroyed in the process.

3. **Expect the emotional crash.** This will take a lot out of you. You will lose sleep. You will feel awful. So give yourself a break. Plan some time off. Take a break.

4. **Hang in there.** The processes around significant events, error, mistakes and failure can be long and arduous. Take care of yourself but don't give up. This issue will get resolved over time. Keep your support structures in place. Keep going. Don't give up!

5. **Work out the learning with support.** Find friends and colleagues who can help you think through what happened, suggest alternatives you could try in the future and help to improve your work or practice as a result.

In short – be honest; be kind; look after yourself; look after others.

Questions Asked

Are there acceptable failures in healthcare?

Yes – we should become better at piloting ideas and experimenting with different ways of doing things. It may be that, especially in toxic cultures, people just want to turn up and do their job – they fear trying new and improved ways of doing things. We need to be better at acceptable failure.

You've mentioned that the way a parent responds to a child's failures affects whether a child develops a fixed or a growth mindset. Do you think that this could also be true of other relationships and in the workplace as well?

This is an excellent question. I think we have to assume that we can. When an unacceptable failure happens, the outcome will depend on not just whether the person involved has a fixed mindset or a growth mindset, it will also depend on whether the person undertaking the investigation has a fixed mindset or a growth mindset. This is because someone undertaking the investigation who has a growth mindset will start from the premise, "I'm sure you didn't wake up this morning intending for this incident to happen. What happened and why?" The investigator should view any failure as a tool that the organisation and the individual can learn from and work to understand how best this is done. Fixed mindset and growth mindset is not just about the person or people involved in the incident, it is probably also about the mindset of the people responsible for managing failures and incidents.

Do you have any particular strategies to help people to fail well?

The problem is that because we are, as a society, so success orientated, there has been little thinking about how we learn well through failure. What I have started to do is invite people together who were involved in an incident and start those meetings with a phrase like "Thank you all for coming. This has happened. I work from a standpoint that none of us got out of bed in the morning with the intention that this would happen. Therefore, we need to understand why this happened, when we are all doing the jobs we are doing because we want good outcomes." None of us wake up in the morning with the intention of arguing with our spouse, or upsetting our children, or scraping the car. But these things happen and if we want to reduce them happening, we need to understand why they have happened. We don't want our colleagues to be defined by their failures by themselves or by others and so we need to support them, and we need to protect their reputations.

"Success consists of going from failure to failure without loss of enthusiasm." Attributed to Winston Churchill.

"Success is not final; failure is not fatal. It is the courage to continue that counts." Attributed to Winston Churchill.

References

1. Grimes C. The Role of Emotions on Learning in Surgical Training: Imperial College, London; 2014.

2. Cannon MD, Edmondson, A.C.. Failing to Learn and Learning to Fail (Intelligently). *Long Range Planning* 2005; **38**: 299-319.

3. Cyert RM, March JG. A behavioral theory of the firm. Englewood Cliffs, N.J.,: Prentice-Hall; 1963.

4. Dweck CS. Mindset. London: Robinson; 2012.

5. Sitkin SB. Learning through Failure: The Strategy of Small Losses. *Research in Organizational Behavior* 1992; **14**: 231-66.

6. Destin M, Svoboda RC. A brief randomized controlled intervention targeting parents improves grades during middle school. *J Adolesc* 2017; **56**: 157-61.

7. Haimovitz KD, C.S. Parents' Views of Failure Predict Children's Fixed and Growth Intelligence Mind-Sets. *Psychological Science* 2016; **27**(6): 859-69.

8. Wang Y, Jones BF, Wang D. Early-career setback and future career impact. *Nat Commun* 2019; **10**(1): 4331.

9. Edmondson A. The Fearless Organisation: Creating Psychological Safety in the Workplace for Learning, Innovation and Growth. New Jersey: John Wiley & Sons; 2019.

10. Kohn LT, Corrigan JM, Donaldson MS. To Err Is Human Building a Safer Health System. Washington: National Academies Press,; 2000. p. 1 online resource (312 p.).

11. Flin R, O'Connor P, Crichton M. Safety at the Sharp End: a Guide to Non-Technical Skills. Farnham: Ashgate Publishing Ltd; 2013.

12. Reason JT. The human contribution: unsafe acts, accidents and heroic recoveries. Farnham, England; Burlington, VT: Ashgate; 2008.

13. Edmondson A. Strategies for Learning from Failure. *Harvard Business Review* April 2011.

14. Cope J. Entrepreneurial learning from failure: An interpretative phenomenological analysis. *Journal of Business Venturing* 2011; **26**: 604-23.

15. Scott SD, Hirschinger LE, Cox KR, McCoig M, Brandt J, Hall LW. The natural history of recovery for the healthcare provider "second victim" after adverse patient events. *Qual Saf Health Care* 2009; **18**(5): 325-30.